NADINE'S FEASTS

Volume 1

BY NADINE ABENSUR

PHOTOGRAPHY BY KAREN HARTNELL-BEAVIS

TRAJECTORY BOOKS

Introduction

I hope you enjoy these recipes. Some of them are old favourites revisited, slightly tweaked, some are new.

A couple of years ago, after 11 years of running an art gallery, ***artpiece gallery***, near Byron Bay in Australia, I moved to Paris to be with my darling, a man I had met at university 42 years previously. For the first time in a very long time, I found myself both with a lot of time on my hands and a fabulous fruit and vegetable market, right downstairs.

I became completely obsessed with cooking. It was so lovely to have someone to cook for! And after many years of living in a place where just about everyone follows some sort of exclusion diet, it was wonderfully refreshing to be with a man who absolutely couldn't care less about such things. The freedom of it!

Slowly, I started to post amateurish pictures of my cooking on Instagram, taken with a very basic iphone but it gave me the freedom to write about the food I was making. I called it: "Love Stories from a Small Kitchen". (And the kitchen really is tiny - 2.5m x 1.5m). It was just the catalyst I needed.

A few months into all this, I travelled to London for a few weeks and participated in a half-day photography workshop with Ros Atkinson from @her_dark_materials It was a gorgeous afternoon and I met some lovely, super-creative people, including a talented photographer, Karen Hartnell-Beavis. Funny, how you get a feeling about things, isn't it? I had a hunch that I would be seeing her again! And indeed I have.

And so, we met again in February 2020, still blissfully unaware of the limitations Covid 19 would impose. I spent a week at her home in Shropshire, cooking my little heart out while she photographed everything. We'd never worked together before but it was easy from the first moment and I'll always be grateful to her and her lovely family for their warm welcome and for this marvelous opportunity. It was such a buzz.

We thought we might turn it all into a book, say hello to our friends and meet new people through it. And so we have and here it is. I hope it's the first of many.

Most of these recipes have been tested and written up while in lockdown, two of us in one small room. I must say that ironically, it made me feel like I never wanted lockdown to end – I just enjoyed the process so much, cooking, eating, writing, day after day.

Contents

Feasting with Friends

Roasted Long Red Peppers with Aubergines

A plate of roasted vegetables you'd find anywhere between Venice and Tripoli, with a somewhat Lebanese sauce, done according to my taste.

Aubergines, red peppers, roasted garlic and a yoghurt, tahini sauce. I loved roasted, grilled, smoked and wood- fired vegetables long before they became the height of fashion, and I will love them long after.

One of the great things about them, and about serving them this way, is that you can go all out, be as abundant as you like, the plate heaped high, the table heaving generously with variety, colour, contrasting and complementary textures and flavours, the sauces and salsas fiery or floral, mild or astringent. Fingers are as acceptable as knives and forks.

You can add nuts and seeds, dried fruit and if you are wise about it, fresh fruit too. There can be flat breads and round loaves, sourdough and soda, cornbread and tortillas – and all of it will work. Lose your fear of oil, embrace garlic and cumin, sumac and sesame, coriander and parsley, berries and cherries (sour of course) and play, just play.

In the recipe that follows, all the vegetables are simply placed on a tray, doused in olive oil and bunged into the oven for 35 - 40 minutes. Leave all notions of al dente behind and understand that the point of these is to be soft, sweet in their own slowly released sugars. Make sure your vegetables are super fresh, firm skinned and glossy.

I'll have to leave for another time, flame smoking, grilling and barbecuing, all of which you can do, instead of roasting, if you have the means to do so!

Roasted Long Red Peppers with Aubergines

Serves 6

Ingredients

3 medium aubergines, cut in half along the length

6 long red peppers, left whole

3 red onions, peeled and cut into quarters

2 whole heads garlic

3 – 4 tbs olive oil

3 long red chillis, left whole

1 tbs cumin seeds

1 tbs balsamic vinegar or pomegranate molasses

sea salt and freshly ground black pepper

handful fresh coriander

plus - not pictured

6 whole medium courgettes, left whole

3 bulbs fennel, cut into quarters

Method

Preheat the oven to 200°c/fan 180°c/gas 6.

Place all vegetables on a large tray – you will probably need two.

Make a dressing of the olive oil, balsamic vinegar or pomegranate molasses, sea salt and freshly ground black pepper and pour all over the vegetables using your hands if necessary to make sure they are all well coated, paying particular attention to the cut side of the aubergines.

Make sure the vegetables are not too crowded in the tray and are all placed cut side down.

Roast for 35 - 40 minutes. The pepper skins should blacken, at least in places, blister and burst, the aubergines should be browned and caramelised, the fennel golden and tender, even charring in places, without being considered burnt, the courgettes, soft right through, the red onion, also slightly charred (if it's cooking too fast, remove it before the rest) and the garlic starting to ooze its pungent juices, skins flaking.

Tahini

Sometimes I come early to the party, sometimes late. And sometimes both. Tahini, the grey, Armenian sesame seed paste, was such a staple of first-wave vegetarian cooking that I eventually grew tired of it and for many years avoided it altogether. As a pivotal component of houmous and baba ghanoush, I understood it very well but on its own, I found it cloying and even a little off-putting. Luckily, I discovered early that loosening it with almost boiling water lightened the effect quite considerably. Cold water, of course, congeals its natural fats and turns it to unmanageable lumps.

I found that orange is its natural ally, garlic, parsley and chives too, and better still, that yoghurt, preferably thick and rich, softens and lengthens it. Even so, when the second wave vegetarian craze for it hit the insta-food tribe, my heart sank a little. Been there, done that, I thought at first, then one fine day, never one to shun the zeitgeist, I found myself reaching for a jar on the supermarket shelf. So here I am making the most of it again, at least for now. Dealt with as described above, it dresses all manner of vegetables, most typically aubergines and courgettes.

Yoghurt, Tahini and Many Herbs

Ingredients

3 tbs tahini

6 tbs greek yoghurt

6 tbs hot water and more if necessary

2 small cloves garlic, very finely chopped

1 x 2 inch piece long, red chili, seeds removed, very finely chopped

juice of 1 orange

handful of cranberries

handful parsley, coriander and/or chives, finely chopped

Method

Start by diluting the tahini with the hot water and stir in the remaining ingredients, the herbs last.

Chermoula

It's worth remembering this freshly made version, busting with herbs, as opposed to the dried spice version you'll buy in plastic sachets. There's frankly no comparison.

When I say large bunches, I mean very large because in Australia these are what I am used to and I mean that there are equal quantities of parsley and coriander. If your own bunches are the standard size, adjust the spices accordingly, that is reduce slightly.

Serves 6

Ingredients

1 large bunch coriander, stalks removed, roughly chopped

1 large bunch parsley, stalks removed, roughly chopped

5 large garlic cloves, very finely chopped

1 tbs cumin, ground

1 tbs sweet paprika

1 tsp harissa

½ long red chilli, very finely chopped

juice of ½ to 1 lemon, depending on size

150 ml olive oil

salt to taste

Method

First stir about half the olive oil into the ground cumin and paprika to make a paste, then add the remaining ingredients, including the remaining oil, and stir.

Although the chermoula keeps in a sealed jar in the fridge for a few days, it is much better made and eaten very fresh as the herbs will otherwise suffer the blackening effect of oxidisation.

To serve

Place the roasted peppers, courgettes and aubergines on a large plate, the yoghurt and tahini sauce and the chermoula by the side, some underneath the vegetables, or on top, in separate bowls or not – it's up to you.

Photo: *From top left, gozleme, roasted cherry tomatoes, roasted vegetables with yoghurt, tahini & many herbs, chermoula in the jar*

Gozleme

For me, who loves the concoction of words as much as the concoction of ingredients, one of the most enjoyable aspects of learning about the food of other cultures, is learning a new vocabulary. It's especially fun when the word has rhythm and cadence, as I thought this did while I still erroneously believed it to be pronounced *Goz-lé-mé*. Unfortunately for me, I've since found out that the word is actually pronounced *Goz-lem*, like Gollum which is a shame – but the point still stands!

You'll find flatbreads in the cooking of many Mediterranean and Middle Eastern cultures and this Turkish version is one of my favourites. I've watched stall holders in London and Paris, Sydney and Melbourne (not, sadly, Istanbul), roll them out fast and thin as you like, an eighth of a turn at a time, achieving a perfect oval before flinging onto a hot plate and adding a filling chosen from an array in front of my hungry eyes.

I don't claim to go as fast, nor to roll as thinly, though I do my best as it is important for the edges to remain thin when folded over, but in my defense, I add two, three times more filling, a deviation I'm happy with. Just make sure that you fry long enough to cook the dough through.

The yeast gives rise (couldn't resist), to a light and airy dough but requires only a 30 minute prove, can be made in a stand mixer with a dough hook attachment and then must be kneaded till smooth as a baby's bottom, no lumpy flesh here thank you very much. Rolling with a chapatti pin, the rolling pin that's tapered at both ends, on a stone, stone like, or marble surface will give best results.

And you can shout this from the rooftops, or keep to yourself the fact that you can also make the dough in a bread machine, or cheat of cheats, use ready-made, shop bought Pizza dough, rolled out more thinly and few will call you out.

Gozleme

Serves 6

Ingredients

For the Gozleme dough

270g plain flour

3 tbs greek yoghurt

1/2 tsp baking powder

1/2 tsp dry yeast

1/2 tsp sea salt flakes

2 tbs olive oil

150ml warm water

extra flour for dusting

Filling

1 smallish red onion, diced

1 clove garlic, very finely chopped

500g baby spinach leaves, stalks trimmed

125g feta, roughly broken up

chilli flakes, a pinch, optional

nutmeg, a pinch

olive oil for frying, about 1/2 tbs per gozleme

salt and pepper

Method

In a large bowl, combine all the ingredients for the Gozleme except the olive oil. Mix with a spoon or fingers until just combined. Turn onto a surface dusted with flour and knead for a few minutes until very smooth. If you feel the dough is too tough, use a little extra water and continue to knead until the dough ball is smooth and comes cleanly away from the sides.

Return to the bowl, cover with a tea towel and set in a warm corner for about 30 minutes to prove. The dough should have doubled in size. Add the olive oil and knead again to get a smooth ball of dough. Cover and set aside for another 30 minutes.

Divide the dough into 6 balls. Roll each dough ball into a large oval. Dust with extra flour as needed to avoid sticking. Roll it as thinly as you can without tearing it. You should be able to see your hand when you place it underneath.

While the dough has been rising, you will have made your filling:: Thinly slice the red onion and fry in a little olive oil til beginning to brown and even crisp a little. Add the finely chopped garlic, nutmeg and chilli flakes. Transfer to a plate, retaining any excess oil in the pan.

In the same pan, add the spinach and cook for a minute or so, first on medium heat till wilted, then on high to cook off excess liquid. Even so, you will need to squeeze it almost dry, only now season with salt and pepper..
Return the onion mix to the pan with the spinach, allow it to cool a little before adding the crumbled Feta.

To assemble

Roll out one ball at a time, til thin, as described above. Place a generous amount of filling in the centre, making sure that you allow at least a 4 cm bare ridge all the way around. Brush this lightly with water on one half and fold over to meet the other. Press down to seal.
Lightly dust the Gozleme with flour and use your rolling pin to gently flatten the whole thing. I tend to prefer to pound rather than roll it.. It can double and even triple in size. The filling will spread but if you've left enough of a gap, that will be fine and your Gozleme should not tear. Mind you, even if it does, you can easily patch it up with a little more dough.

Brush a large frying pan with a little olive oil and fry the Gozleme on each side for a couple of minutes till a well burnished bronze, tinged with occasional charred patches. Cut into triangles or quarters and serve hot, either on their own or as part of a feast. Lemon wedges by the side are always appreciated.

A Family Feast

Roasted Vegetable Tagine with Chickpeas and Muscatel Raisins

I currently live in Paris for at least half the year, so it's been something of an eating fest for me. I've gone a bit mad for Patisserie and for the first few months at least, I also went pretty nuts over the dozens of North African restaurants here. Yet not one, so far, has given me food at all like that of my childhood in Casablanca. The Tagines of my childhood were richer, more slowly cooked, incredibly refined (this isn't just the rantings of an old person suffering from nostalgia). Some members of my family were particularly good cooks I know, but there's no excuse really – it isn't that hard! Watching my mother's aunts cooking and laughing together remains one of my happier early memories. And the things that emerged out of their kitchens would blow your minds now, as it blew mine then.

But neither is this Tagine typical, since it's entirely vegetable based. I have made one significant change by adding a tomato-based sauce to it, in deference to the Algerian versions usually served in Paris. All the same, it does have the richness I am used to and prefer.

It's best to make the tomato preparation first, ladle it into your Tagine dish and then add the roasted vegetables carefully to it, so they don't disintegrate into an indistinct mush. You then scatter some of the chickpeas and raisins on top and serve at once.

You can make this recipe in a normal large saucepan – the word 'tagine' after all, means just that. However, if you are seduced by the rustic quaintness of the conical lid, take this precautionary step first; If your tagine is unglazed, it's wise to soak it in the bath overnight. By expanding the terracotta and increasing its moisture content, you can reduce the risk of cracking. Bear in mind that in Morocco, tagines were – and in some places still are - made by peasant women, crouching on stools by the side of the road. At only a few dhirams each, the duty of care is almost redundant. As a tagine cracks, it is simply thrown back on the pile of clay, soaked till soft and re - used. Contemporary stainless steel bottomed tagines with beautifully glazed lids are not as authentic but they do the job.

Here are some optional but desirable serving suggestions: 200ml thinned Greek yoghurt, chopped herbs aplenty, a finely chopped garlic clove, all mixed together makes a delicious drizzle and you can elevate ordinary flour tortillas, by frying half a dozen of them in a little very hot olive oil for a minue on both sides, til golden brown and puffy as pillows. And you can also have the Chermoula (See Page 13) by the side if you like.

Roasted Vegetable Tagine with Chickpeas and Muscatel Raisins

Serves 4 - 6

Ingredients

150 ml olive oil, quite fruity if possible

8 cloves garlic, 6 peeled but left whole, the rest finely chopped

6 - 8 golden shallots, peeled and either left whole or cut in half

3 smallish fennel bulbs, cut into 6

1.2 kg pumpkin, peeled and cut into pieces 5cm x 3 cm

2 aubergines, not too large, cut just as the pumpkin

2 1/2 long red chillis, 2 left whole, plus half, very finely chopped

1 can cooked chickpeas, reserve the liquid

1 can chopped tomatoes

250ml very hot vegetable stock (out of a packet or home made)

good fat pinch saffron, infused in the hot stock, above

2tbs ground cumin

1/2 tsp ground cinnamon

2 tbs sweet paprika

small handful each of parsley and coriander

75g muscatel raisins, or yellow raisins

tabasco

sea salt and freshly ground black or white pepper

Method

Preheat the oven to 200°C/Fan 180°C/Gas 6

First bring your stock to the boil. Transfer it to a jug, into which you have added a fat pinch of saffron and let it infuse for a good 15 minutes, til the stock turns to a rich amber.

Baste the pumpkin, fennel, aubergine and whole chillis generously in about half the olive oil, season with salt and pepper and a splash of Tabasco. Roast in the oven for 25 - 30 minutes or til tender, golden and slightly charred all over. The aubergine and pumpkin and chillis can share a tray, but ideally the fennel should go in separately as it will take a little longer than the rest.

In a bowl, toss the strained chickpeas in about a teaspoon each of the cumin and paprika, a little salt and pepper and add them to the roasting vegetables. As an aside, if you prefer the chickpeas dry roasted and crisp, roast them separately, without oil!
A good compromise is to do half one way and half the other, so that there are a few crispy ones to add to the herbs and raisins you will later scatter on top.

Meanwhile heat the remaining olive oil in a large saucepan. Sautée the shallots on quite a high heat, moving the pan about to prevent burning, til they are transparent and a rich gold which will take about 10 minutes.

Then add the whole garlic cloves and sauté again adding a little of the saffron stock to aid their softening and prevent them from burning. Keep adjusting heat and liquid as necessary.

To these, now add the cumin, cinnamon and paprika, stirring all the time and add about another ladle of stock. The spices should start to form a paste with the stock and the shallot's own juices. Keep stirring, keep adding the stock, a little at a time, the sauce becoming thicker and richer as it absorbs the spices and the shallots break down and fall apart. Add the chopped garlic now.

Add the can of tomatoes and cook the whole lot together for about 5 minutes. You can also add about half the reserved chickpea water at this stage and simmer for another minute or two.

If you are using a tagine, now is the time to transfer this already dangerously delicious sauce to it; a rich, soupy base for the vegetables to follow.

If you have a heat diffuser, place it on a soft flame and place the tagine on top. If not, just turn the flame down really low and be vigilant. Carefully transfer the roasted vegetables onto it, layering them with the firmer fennel first, then the pumpkin and finally the aubergines. Pour over any remaining hot saffron stock and gently stir half the chickpeas through, retaining some to scatter over, as described above.

It's quite ok for some of the pumpkin and aubergine to break up a little to add to the rich body of the tagine but you do want most of it to retain its shape and texture.

Simmer gently like this for about 5 minutes, adjusting the heat as you see fit, so increasing it, if all seems too watery, or decreasing, if it seems too thick. You can also add a little more stock, or chickpea water to keep the whole thing moving - neither too dry, nor too wet is the way.

Season with salt and pepper, scatter the muscatel raisins over and add the parsley and coriander just before serving, so that both maintain, their lively, herbaceous freshness.

A Pilaf with Broad Beans, Muscatel Raisins, Fresh Cardamom and Pistachios

The title of this recipe could have been an essay in itself for there is quite a lot more to it than described there. You will also be adding saffron and cumin, in ground and seed form, shallots, masses of them, fried golden brown, garlic and cinnamon, chilli, parsley and coriander aplenty. Add to this the sweet nuttiness of the basmati rice, olive oil and lemon zest and you are in for an aromatic treat - multilayered fragrance wafting through the house.

Once upon a time, when I was very young, my pilafs were made differently, the rice boiled separately, then added to the pan of fried onion, spice and herbs. But you live and learn that old habits stand in the way of the new and the better, so one fine day you give them up and life opens up. The kitchen is a great laboratory for this lesson.
So here, the rice is added to the fried onion and only then is the stock added, so that by the time the rice is cooked, it needs only to be gently moved around in the pan a few times using a thin edged wooden or rubber spoon, so every grain takes on a golden hue and rounded fragrance, while remaining fluffy and light.

And now, by way of etymology, a short history lesson. Pilaf is mentioned in the legends of Alexander the Great, as a dish served in the royal court of what is now Afghanistan. Taking the recipe as a spoil of war back to Macedonia, pilaf became a national dish of Greece and then of Persia, adopted by communities in Turkey and Greece and spread further afield by the Jews of Central Asia and Persia, the name going through several iterations reflecting these migrations. You may have seen it as Pilau, Plov, Pilav, Pulao and if you are well travelled, many other names besides but essentially it is the same recipe, always a fried onion base, frequently an added meat. Broad beans are a common addition, golden raisins feature often and there is usually a nut, almond or pistachio. Sometimes it is cooked stove - top as here and in some places, only the oven prepared version is considered accurate. Sometimes, it is topped with a thick layer of yoghurt and sometimes with real silver leaf. So when you make this, you are participating in a long and illustrious culinary tradition in which you have plenty of room to play.

A final word: I cook this in a large frying pan and easily get away with the larger than usual recommended volume of stock, it evaporating faster on the wider surface area.

A Pilaf with Broad Beans, Muscatel raisins, Fresh Cardamom and Pistachios

Serves 4

Ingredients

225g shallots, peeled and thinly sliced
225g basmati rice
500 ml hot water made into a stock with
a fat pinch of saffron
50 ml olive oil
2 garlic cloves, finely sliced
1 tbs cumin seeds
½ tsp cumin, ground
4 cardamom pods, crushed, seeds only
1 cinnamon stick
200g frozen broad beans (fresh in the brief season when you can), blanched for 4 minutes in lightly salted boiling water
35g muscatel or golden raisins, soaked in a little saffron stock for a few minutes
30g pistachios, roasted and salted, weighed in shell or 15g shelled weight
flat leaf parsley and coriander to make up one generous handful, roughly chopped
sea salt flakes and freshly ground black pepper

Method

Make up the stock in a jug by pouring very hot water over the large pinch of saffron strands and letting it stand for at least 15 minutes. It should be ready to go, that is a gorgeous amber, by the time it's time to cook the rice.

So: Heat the olive oil in a large frying pan and when hot, fry the shallots, stirring regularly for about 15 minutes, til they are a deep golden brown, caramelising in their own sugars. You may need to add splatters of hot stock, now and then to keep the shallots moving, to raise the temperature, as the liquid hits the pan and releases steam, thus softening them more quickly, so that they don't burn before they are properly softened, adding the chopped garlic, ground cumin and cumin seeds, crushed cardamom seeds, salt and pepper about half way through. The result will be rich and jammy and form the basis of the Pilaf.

Then blanch the broad beans, drain, refresh under cold water and slip off the skins to reveal the lush, verdant green of the bean. Set aside.

Add the rice to the frying pan. On a medium heat, stir into the spiced onion mix to coat all over, to impart spice to every grain. Cover with the stock, bring to the boil, then reduce to a medium heat and cover with a well fitting lid.

14 minutes later the rice will be perfectly cooked. Switch off the heat but keep the pan on the ring while you incorporate the broad beans, raisins and at the last minute, the pistachios and herbs. Let rest for a few minutes. Then serve at once if you can.

Lunch in a Jar

Roasted Vegetables with Cumin, Lime and Harissa Dressing

The dressing comes from **'enjoy'** (Harper Collins UK, Lantern Press Australia, 2005) the last book I wrote and it's one I use often. The carrot salad it dressed then also had pecan nuts and a wonderful, feta–like goat's cheese, so feel free to add these to the vegetables.

It's important that none of the pieces end up too large – you want them to fit snuggly in the jar. A medium sized preserving jar is ideal and you really can cram in the vegetables, a layer at a time, as long as the carrots stand tall and protrude from the jar like an exotic floral arrangement!

The idea for the roasted vegetables (and everything else) in a jar came many years ago when I was running my art gallery (**art piece gallery**), in Mullumbimby, near Byron Bay, Australia.

I would often take clients to visit artists in their studios and because many of them already knew me as a cookery writer and all of them had only the most rudimentary cooking facilities, I got into the habit of taking lunch along with me. My favourite goat's cheese came in charming, squat, glass jars and I'd accumulated boxes of them.

Without really thinking about it, I began to fill them with all sorts of things, some made especially for the occasion and some straight out of the fridge.

There'd often be pesto in one, a rich salsa in the other, chickpeas in a rich sauce, the goats cheese of course, and one day, a pile of roasted vegetables from the previous evening's supper. There were olives and salad, sometimes rice or quinoa, in short all the bits for an arty lunch, balanced on milk crates or paint-splattered drop cloths, no plates, or serving dishes required. I wasn't much of a bread maker then but a friend of mine was and so I took along her utterly divine rye sourdough. And to complete the picture, there was always either a chocolate mousse, or my homemade chocolate truffles.

Anyway, those lunches became "a thing". I don't suppose there are too many art gallery directors who show up with a basket of jars full of food to the studio but I was one.

More recently, in my diminutive Parisian apartment, I've revived the habit. A dinner for friends entailed the very meal you are about to see.

Quinoa 'Taboulish', Roasted vegetables in a jar, roasted garlic and chermoula

Roasted Vegetables in a jar with Cumin, Lime and Harissa Dressing

Serves 6

Ingredients

For the Roasted Veg

500g baby carrots, small, firm, assorted colours

3 small red onions, cut into quarters

3 small bulbs fennel, cut into 6 segments each

6 garlic cloves, left whole

1 tbs cumin seeds

1 tsp ground cumin

1 tbs maple syrup

pinch cinnamon, optional

60 ml extra virgin olive oil

dash tabasco, about half a teaspoon

sea salt and freshly ground black pepper

For the Lime and Cumin Vinaigrette

1 garlic clove, finely chopped

grated zest of 2 limes

2 - 3 tbs fresh lime juice

1 spring onion, finely chopped

1/2 red chilli, finely chopped

1/2 tsp cumin seeds, lightly toasted and partly pounded

1/2 tsp coriander seeds, lightly toasted and pounded

1/4 tsp dijon mustard

60ml olive oil

2 tbs chopped parsley

1 tsp harissa

sea salt

Method

Preheat the oven to 200°C./fan 180°C./gas 6

Put all the vegetables, including the garlic cloves into a tray large enough that they have space to move, or use two separate trays if you need to. You do not need to peel the carrots. Their shriveled, puckered skins when roasted is part of the appeal. Add the spices with the tablespoon of maple syrup and the 60 ml of olive oil to the vegetables and toss to coat. You can use a wooden spoon or your hands to do this.

Roast for 30 – 35 minutes til tender, gently caramelised and even a little charred in places.

While the vegetables are roasting, assemble your dressing by placing all the ingredients in a jar and shaking to combine.

Douse the roasted vegetables in about half the dressing before cramming into the jar and serve extra dressing in a small jar by the side.

Quinoa 'Taboulish'

Ok, the title gives the game away. This is kind of like Tabouleh though the fact that it's made with quinoa isn't the only sacrilege. There are no tomatoes but there are cranberries, no raw onion but plenty roasted, no mint (though you could) but plenty of garlic, yet still it's herby and summer fresh and great as a side with Houmous and Tahini, with fat, soft, tomatoey butterbeans or broadbeans in cumin and paprika, with Greek yoghurt and charred courgettes, with pickled vegetables and beetroot or with lime dressed roasted baby carrots and it's a salad but you can eat it with a spoon.

Just as I make Pilaf in a large frying pan, I like to do this in the same way. It allows me to fry the grain evenly first (not that quinoa is a grain, just looks like one - in fact, it's the seed of a flowering plant in the Amaranth family). It's a cute little thing when cooked, splitting apart into a small core with a Saturnian ring.

I must say that I used to feel extremely uneasy about Quinoa because of its adoption by the Western health food brigade. In appropriating the small production, from its Andean source, an entire ecology was affected, both environmentally and socially, and even nutritionally, as the indigenous population turned to a less healthy Western diet, the wealthier they became from the new levels of production. Now that production is world wide, European as well as Asian and American, I've accepted it as part of my cooking arsenal. That's the reality.

Quinoa 'Taboulish'

Serves 2 - 4

Ingredients

200g quinoa, preferably mixed, red, white and black

500 ml water, very hot

2 tbs olive oil, divided

1 red onion, peeled and cut into thin wedges and fried in a little olive oil

1 garlic clove, finely chopped

¼ tsp siracha or tabasco

3 cardamom pods, outer husk removed, seeds pounded

½ tbs cumin seeds

saffron, a pinch, immersed in the hot water above for 15 minutes till turned to an amber coloured stock

30g pistachios, salted and roasted, 15g shelled weight

50g cranberries

juice of half a lime

1 large handful coriander, tough stalks removed

1 large handful flat leaf parsley, tough stalks removed

long red chilli, 7 cm piece, seeds removed, finely chopped

sea salt and freshly cracked black pepper

Method

Heat half the olive oil in a large frying pan and when hot, add the quinoa to the pan. Fry on a medium heat for 3-4 minutes with the chopped garlic, crushed cardamom seeds, cumin seeds, chilli sauce, salt and pepper, til well coated, then immediately add all the hot Saffron stock, turn the heat down to medium, cover with a lid and simmer for 15 minutes, til all the stock is absorbed and the quinoa is tender, its outer ring separated from the core. More often than not, I ask you to cook things, especially grains, longer than packet instructions suggest.

Transfer to a bowl and mix with the cranberries, fried or roasted red onion, all the herbs, the remaining spoonful of olive oil and the lime juice. Finally scatter with the pistachios and serve.

Date and coconut salsa
- see next page for recipe

Date and Coconut Salsa

I call this a salsa but I've also called it a salad and a relish. And somehow, none of these words quite do it. It's somewhere in between I think.

The recipe comes originally from Claudia Roden's seminal **'The Book of Jewish Food'**, and I made it for so many years that I also included it in my book **'enjoy'** (Harper Collins UK, Lantern Press Australia, 2005, now available online), with fresh, as opposed to desiccated coconut. When I was making it for this recipe, I couldn't get hold of Tamarind, so I added atypical cranberries instead and they worked, not only in terms of sour sweet tartness but the pretty colour only served to improve matters. New habit formed right there.

Though it is usually an accompaniment to fish, I think it goes very well with grilled and fried vegetables, and goes well with mild tasting cheese 'Borekas' – little deep fried pastry triangles, ricotta being the most suitable filling because of its intrinsic sweetness.

In the original recipe, the ingredients are pounded to a paste. In my version, the ingredients are roughly chopped and only lightly pounded to retain, texture, colour, and zappy freshness. I serve it with mini, deep fried papadams for a cute canapé to precede a curry or couscous, and it's gorgeous here with the pilaf and roasted veg.

Ingredients

125g desiccated coconut, unsweetened or about half a brown coconut,
brown outer shell and skin removed and flesh coarsely grated
a large bunch of coriander
10 - 12 pitted medjool dates
juice of 2 limes
2 tbs cranberries, half pounded to a rough paste with a tablespoon of boiling water, the rest left whole
2 garlic cloves, very finely chopped
1/2 tsp sea salt
1/2 a long red chilli, deseeded and chopped to a confetti

Method

If using desiccated coconut, pour 150ml of warm water over the coconut to soften it, about 15 - 20 minutes.

Cut the roots off the coriander and discard or set aside for another purpose. Roughly chop the rest, then add the remaining ingredients and mix to make a rich and chunky relish/salad/salsa. It does keep for a few days in a sealed jar but is best eaten super fresh, as the coriander tends to oxidise and you lose the appeal of the just-chopped fresh herb.

Breakfast, Brunch, Lunch or Supper

Sunomono - *Cucumber and Seaweed Salad*

On the morning of the day that Macron announced the Coronavirus lockdown in France, I'd walked over an hour from La Motte Piquet Grenelle in the 15[eme] Arrondissement to a little Japanese restaurant in Rue Saint Anne, near Palais Royale just to eat this salad. I'd already been the previous week and I had craved it ever since. As it turned out, it was to be the last thing I ate outside of home before the measures were introduced. It will probably be the first thing I go to when they are lifted.

Not that it's difficult to reproduce at home and if wakame is difficult to find, you can at a pinch replace it with a more easily accessible seaweed. Rich in minerals, especially iodine, it's low in calories and several studies suggest that it helps to reduce blood pressure (don't go overboard on it if yours is low), lowers cholesterol and heart disease risk, that it may decrease blood sugar and improve insulin resistance. It's good for your skin, brain and bones, it's considered anti-inflammatory and more.

You'll often find it in dried form, so that you'll need to soak it in water for 10 -15 minutes first. Across the road from where I live, the local supermarket sells it, emerald green in small tubs ready to eat which given how many things I seek that it doesn't sell, is a small victory.

If you don't know the joy of pickled cucumber and seaweed for breakfast, I'm happy to be the bearer of such glad tidings. If anything sets me up for a good day, this does.

You'll find that a few drops of sesame seed oil go a long way and I never miss out on the pleasing pop of sesame seeds themselves. Anyway, I hope you enjoy the salad's sweet, salty, tangy dressing. Don't expect decorum though: you will want to pick up the bowl and drink the dressing like the life giving elixir it is. I tell you, sugar and all, it rights all wrongs.

Writing up this recipe, inevitably triggered that craving again but – sad face – I had no cucumber, so I took what I had in the fridge: one carrot, a small cheek of fennel and a couple of asparagus spears. I turned the carrots to matchsticks, the fennel to Carpaccio thin slices and the asparagus to ribbons (with my trusted vegetable peeler).

There happened to be a little of the supermarket seaweed too and I try never, ever to be out of sesame seeds or red chili.

So marinating in that drinkable dressing, we had salad for lunch.

Sunomono

Serves 2 – 4

Ingredients

I cucumber or 2 lebanese cucumbers, half peeled in alternating strips

75g ready to eat wakame or 4 tbs dehydrated, soaked for 15 minutes

Dressing

1/2 tsp soya sauce, or tamari

3 tbs rice or other pale, sweet vinegar

1tbs maple syrup, or soft brown sugar or palm sugar

2 cm knob fresh ginger, peeled, grated and squeezed for juice

½ tsp sesame oil, optional

Garnish

1 tbs sesame seeds, half white and if you can find them, half black

1/4 Long red chilli, chopped to confetti

Method

Simply very thinly slice the whole cucumber, or two Lebanese cucumbers, peeled as described above, either with a mandolin or with a vegetable peeler. Sprinkle with a little sea salt – a scant half teaspoon is plenty. Transfer to a sieve placed over a bowl large enough to catch the juices and let it sit there for a good 20 minutes. You can further squeeze out any excess liquid with your hands.

Move the cucumber to a bowl with the soaked wakame, cut into strips and either simply pour all the dressing ingredients over, or place these in a jar first, shake to combine and then pour over the cucumber and seaweed.

Scatter with the sesame seeds and the freshly chopped, long, red chilli.

Though you'll want to eat it at once, it does keep well overnight in the fridge and then has the advantage of being cold – a rare occasion for wishing this on any salad – and especially refreshing.

Garnish with the chilli and sesame seeds.

Okonomiyaki with Crispy Fried Tofu

This is a simple recipe but there is quite a lot to say about it. The first is that it's important to acknowledge that Okonomiyaki is a Japanese street food, sitting comfortably somewhere between omelette, pancake and fritter. It's important to emphasise this because secondly, the mellifluous word famously means: "what you like, grilled". In other words, it is open to all sorts of manipulations and personal interpretations, which is music to my culinary ears. And thirdly, this version stretches the point by doing away with all meat and fish components and replacing them with tofu in all its fancy dress-up garb. You'll see. Before we go on, here's another thing (or two). I was about to begin this sentence with "In an ideal world, you would have Dashi for your stock." Then I realised that the alternative given below is probably a good deal more accessible, probably doesn't require a special trip to the Asian food store and hits the desired Umami complexity. So the ideal world is the one you find yourself in. If you want to be more Japanese about it, soak wakame seaweed together with dried shitake and dried, preserved, fermented bonito flakes. Bring to near boiling and strain.

A Japanese tradition it is good to stick to is the accompaniment of an Okonomiyaki sauce. Whilst you can buy this online, I make my own version, untraditional with its addition of butter (for gloss and rich body) but multi layered, deep flavoured and way, way better I think to the usual alternative – HP sauce!

The other required dressing, the Japanese Kewpie mayonnaise, is, like its brown sauce companion, usually squeezed out of a plastic bottle. I don't know about you but this rather turns me off. So I drizzle the first sauce from a small jug; the mayonnaise, I spoon from its pot. You can use the point of a small knife to streak them together into some sort of grid-like pattern. Or stick to the plastic bottles, if you feel they go better with the laid back, street food vibe.

If you are familiar with Okonomiyaki, you will notice that I have used very much less flour in the mix than usually suggested. It's by design, not accident - this is no place for stodge.

And if, big if, you are by any chance, planning to add Tempura to your Japanese feast, keep back the little bits of batter that are bound to break off into the hot oil. It is a habit to add them to the Okonomiyaki mix. Delicious and crisp as that is, there is no need to go to the trouble of making tempura especially, unless you really, really want to. Your Okonomiyaki will be yummy anyway, even without.

Two of us made a (filling) main meal of these quantities, a plate of sautéed bok choy by the side. What is proposed here however is a feast, the miso aubergines indulgently rich yet surprisingly light. And you can serve all at once, encouraging everyone to share, if not exactly tear at the Okonomiyaki, chopsticks being more the thing than fingers.

Okonomiyaki

A note on how to proceed: First prepare all the ingredients. In the spirit of the Japanese kitchen, have them all weighed up and sitting in bowls or on a tray, so that you can move quickly. Before you start cooking the Okonomiyaki, refer to the recipes below for the stock, for the Okonomiyaki sauce and for the fried tofu.

I suggest you make the Okonomiyaki sauce first. It can cool a little, that's fine but if you are to make it much in advance, then warm it through before using to dissolve the butter which will have re set by then.

Then make the Okonomiyaki mix but set aside for now.
Now fry the tofu and set that aside while you go back to frying the Okonomiyaki itself. I hope that's clear!

Serves 2 - 4

Dashi Stock

Ingredients

2 tsp rice vinegar

1 tsp siracha or chilli sauce

6 - 8 drops fish sauce

1 tsp soya sauce

1 small clove garlic, very finely chopped

water to make up to 100ml

Method

Mix all ingredients together in a jar and stir or shake.

Okonomiyaki

Ingredients

4 eggs

65g plain flour

100ml dashi stock, (see above) cooled

65g raw potato, (1 small), peeled and grated

2 tsp crispy onion, optional

3 fine spring onions, trimmed off toughest green part and chopped

2 tsp fresh ginger, grated and squeezed for its juice alone (or japanese pickled ginger, diced)

250g cabbage, thinly shredded (ideally hispi or sweetheart cabbage)

3 tbs sesame seeds

oil for frying (light olive oil/sesame oil or grape seed oil)

......recipe continued overleaf

recipe continued......

Method

Mix together the egg and flour, then stir in the stock, making sure that there are no lumps.
Add the grated potato to the batter, then stir in the crispy onions, if using, the chopped spring onions, cabbage and squeezed ginger juice.

Heat a thin layer of oil (light olive oil tinged with a few drops of the more powerful sesame seed oil, or grape seed oil is good too) in a frying pan on a medium heat. Pour the mixture into the pan, scatter with half a tablespoon of sesame seeds and fry for five minutes.

The first side cooked, you'll need to turn it out onto a plate then slide it back into the pan for the second side, adding sesame seeds again. A wide egg flipper also does the trick.

Serving straight from the pan keeps it hot. Dress dramatically with the two sauces, the tofu, the seaweed, the chili confetti and serve immediately.

To garnish

kewpie mayonnaise, or regular – about 2 - 3 tbs
okonomiyaki sauce, see mine below
fried tofu, (see below)
2 sheets of nori seaweed, cut in 4 along the length, then snipped into thin strips.
japanese pickled ginger
red chilli, thumb size piece, seeds removed, chopped to confetti

Okonomiyaki Sauce

Ingredients

50g butter
2 tbs tamari or soya sauce
2 tbs maple syrup
fish sauce, several dashes – about ¼ tsp
2 tsp siracha
3 tsp rice vinegar
1 medium tomato

Method

Blanch the tomato in boiling water for one minute, skin and seeds removed and finely chop.

Melt the butter in a small pan and add all the other ingredients. Bring to boiling point, then reduce the heat and simmer for about 8-10 minutes, til reduced to about half, glossy, smooth, thick but still pourable.

Crispy fried Sesame Tofu

Serves 2 - 4

Ingredients

250g firm tofu, cut into ½ cm thick batons, 5 – 6 cm long

2 tbs soya sauce

1 tbs maple syrup

1 tbs brandy

2 tbs water

2 tbs light olive oil

dash siracha or other chilli sauce

1 clove garlic, very finely chopped

ginger, 6 or 7 gratings on the parmesan shaving side of a grater, pulp squeezed for its juice, then discarded

1 tbs sesame seeds, optional

Method

Put all the ingredients, except for the sesame seeds in a pan and let sit for at least 5 minutes but for pretty much as long as you like, even overnight.

Then place over a high heat and bring to a spluttering boil.

Turn down the heat to about half and continue to cook til the liquid is all but evaporated, the tofu well coated in a rich, dark, sticky, caramelised sauce, crisping at the edges and generally looking about as unlike tofu as you can imagine and as un-bland.

Towards the end you can add the tablespoon of sesame seeds and let them sizzle, crackle and pop, sticking to the tofu like a sort of savoury praline.

Set aside while you fry the Okonomiyaki. Serve on top of the Okonomiyaki.

Crispy fried tofu
see previous page for recipe

Haloumi in Maple and Lime Glaze with all kinds of herbs and leaves

Haloumi is the brined, un-ripened, semi hard Cypriot cheese from traditionally unpasteurised, half goat's, half sheep's milk, so many of us love. I explain this because, living in Paris, as I now do, few seem to know it and I had to go a-hunting to finally track it down in a huge Lebanese and Middle Eastern supermarket.

I don't remember if anything in particular triggered this recipe, I just know that I had a friend coming for lunch and I had made the Maple and Miso glazed aubergines. I knew they wouldn't be quite enough on their own, so I grabbed the Haloumi out of the fridge and in 5 minutes (8 when you count roasting the almonds) had this.

In fact, it's important not to fry the Haloumi too long at all (I know because I have). Really, even though Haloumi has a high melting point, it only takes 2 minutes, 3 at most, just so the cheese softens to its elastic best. Any longer and it loses its moisture, tenderness, all its gorgeous malleability. Not good at all. "Like old chicken" said my darling when I'd taken my eye off it too long. I haven't made that mistake again!

But now that the notion is firmly established in my repertoire, I take it further. It is all the better for bitter leaves and herbs. At the very least, think of a medley that includes rocket, Thai basil, coriander and mint. The sauce drenched cheese is rich and sticky, sweet and just a little sour and you'll need only a little each, so a packet can easily serve 4, 6, or at one deliciously molten slice per head, as many as 8. The leaves take up the sauce, lighten and make lunch of it all.

P.S. If you want to stay more culturally true, use a flower scented honey instead of Maple Syrup but anyone who knows me knows that my love of the latter only matches my inexplicable antipathy to the former. Don't blame me - it's a physiological thing. So it's Maple Syrup all the way for me and that's just how it is.

Haloumi in Maple and Lime Glaze with all kinds of herbs and leaves

Serves 4 - 6

Ingredients

250g haloumi – ie 1 standard packet, drained and cut into 8 – 9 slices

1 tbs olive oil

2 tbs maple syrup

1 tsp soya sauce

1 tsp balsamic vinegar

juice of half a lime

½ standard garlic clove, thinly sliced

couple of drops chilli sauce – tabasco or siracha

To serve

1/2 small red onion, peeled and thinly sliced, soused in 1 tablespoon of balsamic vinegar while you prepare the rest

combination of rocket, thai basil, coriander, fresh mint – 1 handful of the mixed leaves per person

40g almonds, blanched in boiling water for 1 minute

½ long red chili, seeds removed, thinly sliced on the diagonal

---

Method

Preheat the oven to 200˚C./fan 180C./gas 6

Prepare the leaves on a serving plate and set aside.

Mix the olive oil, maple syrup, soya sauce, teaspoon of balsamic vinegar, juice of half a lime, thinly sliced garlic and chilli sauce in a deep plate or shallow bowl and in it, rest the slices of Haloumi for about 5 – 10 minutes to macerate.

Meanwhile, place the blanched almonds on a tray and pop them into the oven. Set a timer for 8 minutes and remove them immediately. Let cool a minute.

Now slip the maple marinade into a small frying pan, into which the haloumi slices will later snugly fit. Bring it to the boil, then down to a simmer and let reduce for one minute.

Once you have done so, add the Haloumi and braise (for in effect that is what you are doing) for no more than 2 – 3 minutes on a medium to high heat, lifting the pan off the heat for a moment, if you need to slow things down a little. Add the almonds and half the sliced chilli in the last moments of cooking. The Haloumi will now be coated in a rich, thick glaze.

Slide onto the prepared salad leaves and drizzle all the pan juices over, finishing off with the Balsamic doused onion and the remaining sliced chilli. Serve at once while the cheese is still hot and molten.

The Handmade (Asian) Feast

Miso Maple Glazed Aubergines

I'm embarrassed to say that for many years, I refused all invitations to try these. I had two prejudices to overcome. For one, I've had a life long but complicated relationship with aubergines. I love them but they haven't always returned the favour. "They're too Yin." I've complained, the Ayurvedic doctor's words ringing in my ears. "They bring me out in a rash." "They absorb oil in industrial quantities". I wail. This latter point, by the way, is compensated for by their very low calorific content – all of 25 calories per 100 grams, if you happen to be counting.

Then one day, at my brother's invitation and in a little Japanese restaurant you should go out of your way to try - (though plenty do already, so you must book ahead), I succumbed. Hook, line and sinker - at first mouthful. The mind is a wondrous thing, is it not - open to suggestion, endlessly malleable. I hold the thought that aubergines are my new friend and all is well.

And anyway, the recipe asks for less oil than most, as you'll see.

A further hesitation hovered around Miso but this too, dispelled. This is the pale version, rice rather than soya based, more pink than brown, milder, sweeter and marrying harmoniously with maple syrup (for which, all hail), garlic, lime, ginger and chili. So now, Twickenham, the home of this little gem of a restaurant (Umi FYI), as well as being a global synonym for Rugby, is forever associated in my mind with this recipe. And as it turns out, Miso is chock-a-block with probiotics and brilliant for the digestion,

So old fears, be damned.

A word about the dressing - when kept in a sealed jar, it keeps in the fridge for several weeks. A good thing, as it can also be used on other Asian salads and vegetables, a simple rice dish or a cold noodle salad by the side.

Miso glazed aubergines

Serves 6

Ingredients

For the miso maple glaze

4 tbs white miso

4 tbs maple syrup

½ tbs soya sauce, optional

½ tbs rice vinegar

juice of half a lime

1 small garlic clove, very finely chopped

1 inch piece ginger grated and squeezed for juice

For the aubergines

3 aubergines, medium, firm and glossy skinned

3 tsp light olive oil

dash tabasco

salt and pepper

For the garnish

3 thin spring onions, tough tops and hairy bits chopped off, finely sliced on the diagonal

1 long red chilli, seeds removed and thinly sliced, also on the diagonal

6 small sprigs coriander, very fresh and pert

Method

Mix all the ingredients for the marinade in a bowl and set aside.

Preheat your oven to 200°C/Fan 180°C/Gas 6. Slice the aubergines in half lengthways. Use a sharp knife to score a crisscross into the cut sides of the aubergines, like a Harlequin's costume. Try not to cut all the way through - 1cm is plenty deep enough.

Use most of the oil to baste the cut surface and any remaining oil, use to baste the skin. Season with a little sea salt, a dash of Tabasco or mild Siracha.

Place in the preheated oven for 35 – 40 minutes, till the flesh is soft beneath the skin.

Use a fish slice or other flat implement to turn the aubergine over. It should now be well browned. Baste with one to two tablespoons of the Miso, Maple glaze and return to the oven for a further ten minutes, till the glaze starts to form a thin, bubbling, caramelised membrane.

Remove from the oven and dress with the finely sliced red chilli, sprigs of coriander and fine diagonals of spring onion and serve at once.

Bok choy with sesame seeds, garlic and chilli
see next page for recipe

Bok Choy with Sesame Seeds, Garlic and Chili

Bok Choy, Pak Choy, Pok Choy, no need to get your knickers in a twist over these – they are all pretty much of a muchness and by any name, work in this super quick recipe. Of course, it is intended as an accompaniment to rice or noodle dishes of various complexity, but I can't tell you how many times I have made an entire meal of a bowlful of greens. On account of an innate greed, I have to regularly practice restraint, whether by skipping a meal here and there, or turning to a bunch of greens for supper. Everyone finds a way of maintaining his or her own inner ecology and that's how I maintain mine.

Here is a tip that I refer to in recipe after recipe: I grate the fresh ginger but rather than leave it at that, I then squeeze the juice out of it. You'll be surprised at just how much comes out and I discard the pulp. I just don't like getting the little fibrous bits stuck in my teeth!

Serves 1 (yup that's me) to 4

Ingredients

3 - 4 medium sized bok choy, split in half lengthways

1 tbs light olive oil

2 garlic cloves, peeled and thinly sliced

1/3 tbs ginger juice (about a 2 inch piece)

1/3 tbs soya sauce

hot water to hand, about a ladle

1/3 tbs maple syrup, optional

½ tsp lime juice

1 tbs sesame seeds

½ long red chilli, finely sliced, divided

sprig coriander to serve

Method

Heat the oil in a frying pan for about 30 seconds, at once adding the sliced garlic and sesame seeds. On a high heat, add the bok choy, soya sauce, a splash of water, so the soya sauce doesn't burn, maple syrup if using – it does add to the silkiness of the final thing, the lime juice, ginger juice and half the sliced red chili.

Sautee for 7 - 8 minutes, which is longer than others will tell you but I like the green blade all the more wilted and the white bulbous part very tender. It all adds to the digestability and I've already said that that's half the point. Scatter the remaining chilli and the coriander all over and eat very soon, the pan juices providing all the zing you need.

Handmade Gyozas with a Shitake Mushroom, Cabbage, Sweetcorn and Tofu Filling

I am going to assume you can get Gyoza skins because somewhere not too far from wherever you are, there is bound to be an Asian Supermarket and they will have them. I say this because I am so used to finding them in my local supermarket in England or Australia but many things I take for granted there, I cannot take for granted in Paris. Why it took me so long (a kind of despondency) to go looking for an Asian supermarket is beyond me because I discovered one just a 10 minute walk away. I found my black rice there, tofu (at long last!), lemongrass, decent coconut cream and much more. And Google map in hand, I did the same two days later, finding in a vast Lebanese Emporium, all the Middle Eastern ingredients I also take so for granted. I found Haloumi, filo pastry, Pomegranate Molasses, Rose water, in short all the things I usually have in my pantry and which I have done without for the last 18 months. I love French food – it's in my blood - and I love cooking it, but now, back in my playground, I feel a hundred per cent more at home. I have a typically miniscule Parisian kitchen but the tiny pantry suddenly contains the whole wide world.

The round Gyoza skins come in packets of 36, a fact I only noticed after I had finished making the recipe, having instinctively made exactly enough filling to fill all 36, not a skerric to spare. This turns out to be a very good thing because, even having eaten more than our fair share of them, my darling and I, there are now 2 bags of them in the freezer awaiting friends, or just one of those evenings when taking something straight out of the freezer feels like a little gift. The great thing is that they are as good cooked from frozen as from fresh.

Oh yes and having faffed around in the past, I was delighted to discover from our friend Google that pleating the edges shut is really quite simple and I shall attempt to describe the process.

Finally, this vegan-by-default filling makes a brilliant forcemeat. You can shape it into compact little sausage shapes in the palm of your hand, roll it in breadcrumbs and fry gently till golden. Adding a little raw egg, even some hardboiled egg to the mix will give you a delicious non-meat sausage that doesn't involve any kind of fakery. And that's as much as I'm saying about that, though a second volume of these recipes would no doubt include much more on the subject.

P.S. I like to serve the Gyozas in small bowls, sitting in the dipping sauce, like a salty, sour little soup, rather than just by the side because like most dressings, which this is, I like to drink it at the end. Oh and I meant to say that most often, the filling is left raw but I think it so much more delicious, cooked first.

Handmade Gyozas with a Shitake Mushroom, Cabbage, Sweetcorn and Tofu Filling

Makes 36

Ingredients

36 wonton skins

230g white cabbage, finely shredded

1 very fresh corn on the cob, kernels sliced off the cob

100g shitake mushrooms, tips removed, then quite thinly sliced

200g tofu, crumbled

30 ml sunflower oil, with a few drops sesame oil (optional)

1 tbs sesame seeds

1 tbs soya sauce

1 tsp siracha or other chili sauce, mild

1 garlic clove, peeled and very finely chopped

1 tsp rice or other pale vinegar

2 sprigs coriander, picked off the stalks and finely chopped

For the Dipping Sauce/Drinkable Dressing

2 tbs soya sauce

3 - 4 tbs water, to taste

2 tsp rice vinegar

10 ml ginger juice

¼ tsp siracha

1 spring onion, finely sliced on the diagonal, white and tender green parts only

pinch brown sugar, optional

coriander, 2 sprigs, picked off the stalks

long red chilli, thumb size piece, seeds removed and finely sliced on the diagonal

......recipe continued overleaf

Method

In a large frying pan, heat the sunflower oil (and sesame oil, if using) and when hot, fry the sweet corn kernels and half the seasoning for 5 minutes til they begin to pop, splutter and turn to a deep golden colour. Then add the shredded cabbage, the sesame seeds and the remaining seasoning and on a medium heat, which you may need to adjust as you go, fry for another 5 minutes, adding the shitake mushrooms till they soften and wilt, again about 5 minutes, then the Tofu for a final 2 or 3 minutes. Keep stirring to release emerging and merging juices and aromas.

Allow filling to cool a little, then place in a food processor and blitz for about 20 seconds. It's best to do this in short, sharp pulses til you have a soft but rugged forcemeat that easily shapes in the hand. Transfer to a bowl.

To assemble

When you come to making the Gyozas, be prepared; a bowl of water for your fingers and a tray for the Gyozas by your side.
Take one skin in the palm of your left hand (assuming you are right handed, the other way round, if not).
With your right hand, or vice versa, take a heaped teaspoon of filling, the size of a plum and place it in the centre of the skin.
Dip your index and middle finger in the water and moisten all around the circle's edge. Now bring the half circles together, pressing firmly to seal.
Begin the pleating at one end by pushing into the dough with your left index finger and folding over with your right thumb and right index finger, exactly as if you were making a pleat. Continue to the end.
Place the completed Gyozas on a tray, ready for immediate use, or for freezing. It's best to transfer them to bags, once frozen, so they don't stick to each other.

For the Dressing

Simply mix all liquid ingredients together in a bowl and divide equally between the individual little bowls, garnishing each with a little coriander, sliced spring onion and sliced red chili.

To make the Gyozas

You can either fry the Gyozas in a couple of tablespoons of sunflower oil, mixed with sesame oil, til evenly golden on all sides which means you'll have to turn them over, and then over again. Or you can simply carefully drop them into lightly salted boiling water where they will be cooked in 3 minutes. Either way is good and as I am sure I don't need to say, addictive. Serve 3 each as a starter, or 6 or up to you. You've got plenty to play with.

Feasting Solo

Black Rice with Roasted Butternut, Avocado and Lemongrass Coconut Cream

Well, well: the things you learn from Google. Or at least the kind souls who feed it with fascinating information. On this occasion, I find out from an award winning blog called **Feasting at Home**, that Black rice is also called Forbidden rice, legend having it, that due to its apparent extraordinary health benefits, a group of Chinese noblemen hijacked its production, barred its access to the populace and sold it at extortionate prices to royalty alone. I suppose that said, royalty's dissolute lifestyle had need of the lower calories and better anti-inflammatory and brain-boosting properties!!

The inspiration for this recipe actually came from the better known Black Rice Pudding with its layer of coconut cream and fresh mango, something I make often. There is a recipe for it in **'enjoy'** (Harper Collins UK, Lantern Books Australia). I wanted to make a savoury version, so here is its first cousin. They bear strong family resemblance. In both, the rice is slowly cooked but retains sweet nuttiness and the coconut cream lends luxury to virtuosity.

I make this when risotto seems too rich or when I need a dose of regality in my life. You will, by the way, regale yourself.

Black Rice with Roasted Butternut, Avocado and Lemongrass Coconut Cream

Serves 4 - 6

Ingredients for the rice

75ml coconut oil, or light olive oil, plus 2 tablespoons light olive oil

125g golden shallots, peeled and chopped

525g black rice

1 stick lemongrass

zest and juice of one lime

1 star anise

1 knob ginger, grated and squeezed for juice

1lt vegetable stock

1 tbs soya sauce

Ingredients for the butternut squash etc.

1 1/2 cans x 400 ml coconut cream, or very thick coconut milk, thick top layer set aside for later use

1 butternut squash, about 850g, peeled and cut into 3 cm square chunks

1 large mango, just ripe, optional

1 avocado, ripe but still firm, sliced very finely

2 tbs palm sugar, or soft brown sugar, optional

1 long red chilli, deseeded and finely chopped

3 tbs sesame seeds ,

3 cloves garlic, very finely chopped

dash chilli sauce

juice of 1 lime

sea salt and pepper

to serve

fresh coriander

Method

Preheat the oven to 200˚C/Fan 180˚C/Gas 6

In a bowl, toss the butternut squash pieces in the 2 tablespoons of light olive oil, a little Tabasco and salt and pepper and spread out onto a roasting tray, large enough so the pieces don't touch. Set aside.

About 15 minutes into starting to cook the rice, transfer the butternut squash to the oven and roast for 25 – 30 minutes til not just tender but also sticky with its own sugars.

Before you start making the rice, separate the coconut cream or milk into its liquid and cream parts.
Season the cream part with a fistful of chopped coriander and a thumb of finely chopped red chilli. Don't yet add salt or lime juice – these will go in at the last moment - and set aside.

Heat the remaining oil, bar a couple of spoonfuls in which to fry the mango, if using.
On a medium heat, fry the shallots till translucent and add the black rice, stirring to coat for 5 minutes.

Add the chopped garlic and fry for a further minute before adding the stock, the star anise, the lime zest, the ginger juice and the stick of lemongrass, the first couple of ladles of stock, one at a time, as if you were making risotto, letting them be absorbed by the rice before adding the remaining stock.

Lower the heat and keep simmering gently, stirring regularly, til all the stock is absorbed by the gently swelling rice. The whole process needs to take a good 50 minutes to an hour, so slow it down if the stock is being absorbed too quickly and even add a little more stock or boiling water, if necessary. Towards the end, stir in the liquid part of the coconut milk or cream only and reserve the thick layer on top. The rice should now be glossy, tender to the bite but not soft and the whole thing sloppy without being soupy. In a rather dark and Gothic way, when the rice looks lush and comforting, it is. Add a touch of chilli sauce, or finely chopped chilli and the lime juice.

Set aside for 10 minutes with a lid on to maintain heat, to allow the flavours to develop.

Meanwhile, heat the palm or soft brown sugar in a frying pan. When it's bubbling, carefully drop the mango slices into it and fry for a minute on each side, so they retain shape and texture while turning that irresistible caramel, we all love so much.

Stir the rice one final time and serve gloopily into bowls with the roasted butternut squash, the fried mango slices if using, the sliced avocado, elegantly fanned if you can and the fresh coriander.

Just as you are ready to eat, add a little salt to the coconut cream simply to balance the sweetness and a splash of lime juice for the same reason.

In savoury mode, the cold cream through the hot rice has the same appeal as ice cream on hot pie. You will keep coming back for more.

P.S. A few more tricks to have up your sleeve: you could blend the avocado to a silky, pale green cream with a spoon or two of water, salt and pepper, a little garlic, or you could go multi cultural and drizzle Tahini over and you could give everyone a perfectly poached egg, or a piece of salmon, drizzled with the Miso Glaze on p46 . And just like that, black rice becomes a staple of your pantry.

Spinach Gomae

When I first became vegetarian, 43 years ago, a whole lot of ingredients new to me, entered my student's pantry. There was Tamari and Tahini, Herbamare (a low sodium vegetable salt) and Bragg Liquid Aminos (a condiment, similar to Soya sauce), there were Umeboshi plums (a wonderful, sour Japanese plum). There were all manner of seaweeds, Kelp, Wakame, Nori, Hiziki. And there was Gomasio, a crushed sesame and sea salt mix which you could (and still can) buy ready made but which I quickly learnt to make myself. I used to sprinkle it over pretty much everything, especially green vegetables. Here it is in its authentic Japanese guise made into a dressing and poured over wilted spinach. It's a good thing it's so good for you because it is addictive. If you happen to have, or to find, Umeboshi plums, add a little chopped up to this salad. It will give it an extra buzz.

Ingredients

250g spinach, doesn't have to be baby

½ tbs light olive oil, if using baby spinach

½ tsp sake or sherry

½ tsp mirin

1 ½ tbs soya sauce, or tamari

3 tbs roasted white sesame seeds

1 tbs caster sugar, or soft brown sugar

pinch of salt

Method

If using baby spinach, simply wash, shake out and place in a large frying pan into which you have warmed a half tablespoon of light olive oil and cook over a medium heat til fully wilted.
Remove from the pan and when cool enough to handle, squeeze off excess liquid. Chop roughly and set aside.

If your spinach is tougher with more stalk to it, plunge it in a pan of salted boiling water for one minute, then drain and chop.

Toast the white sesame seeds in a frying pan til they begin to colour and a few start to pop.
Use a pinch of salt to help you to grind them in a mortar and pestle, or the small food processor attachment of a stick blender.

Combine the crushed sesame seeds in a small bowl with the Sake, Mirin, Soya sauce and sugar. Pour over the spinach, mix to coat and serve.

An Everyday French Feast

A Cauliflower and Saffron Velouté with Pan-Popped Corn

I can't bring myself to call this a soup because it is so voluptuous, so velvet-smooth and so rich despite the sparsity of ingredients, that it feels more like eating soufflé than soup. Far be it for me to want to sow divisions but there do seem to be those who like their soups chunky and those who like them smooth and I tend to fall into the latter camp. I love food that feels rich while remaining light and these are definitely things you can say about this velouté, a word that doesn't mean velvety for nothing.

In this recipe, I don't even, as I would have done in the past, bother to sauté the cauliflower first, much less roast it (that'll be another recipe).

I literally just break off and reserve the leaves for another use (think roasted together with split down the middle small potatoes and whole garlic cloves, in a medley of grain mustard and cumin seeds.) The leaves removed, a large cauliflower comes in at about 780g and takes a litre of the saffron stock.

I use Herbamare, a favourite health food product going back to the 70s and just as relevant and effective today. It's a vegetable salt, lower in sodium and with a complex flavour that does away with the need for a stock cube or stock powder. That allows me to drizzle a little of the amber hued oil onto each bowl of soup.

Divide into bowls, with a spoonful of corn carefully atop, a drizzle of saffron oil as finishing touch - and waste not a moment in eating.

A Cauliflower and Saffron Velouté with Pan-Popped Corn

Serves 4

Ingredients

1 whole cauliflower, broken up into florets, leaves removed and reserved

2 whole, peeled garlic cloves

1 litre water, or mild vegetable stock

2 fat pinches saffron, divided

1 whole corn on the cob, kernels sliced off

3 tbs olive oil, divided

small handful parsley

sea salt or herbamare and freshly ground black pepper

Method

For the soup

Divide the cauliflower into florets and plonk them and two whole peeled garlic cloves in a saucepan, large enough to comfortably hold it and the litre of boiling water into which you have first steeped a fat pinch of saffron.

Also add a tablespoon of olive oil, some sea salt, or Herbamare and a pinch of white pepper and that's it. Bring to the boil and keep doing so, till the florets are soft.

For the pan-popped corn

If you start to fry the sweetcorn kernels, pretty much the moment you have set the cauliflower on the boil, both will be ready at the same time.

Heat one tbs of olive oil in a medium sized frying pan. When hot add the corn kernels, season with salt and pepper and fry on a medium heat til the corn starts to brown and caramelise and splutter and pop rather alarmingly. Remove from heat and set aside.

Allow the cauliflower to cool a little before transferring it and the hot liquid into the blender, making sure that you don't overfill the blender – better to do it in two lots if necessary - then blitz and blitz and keep blitzing til the soup is as smooth as smooth can be. You'll know what I mean when I say voluptuous and velvet smooth. Try to resist the temptation to thin it down too much. I want you to experience mousse-like, soufflé-like airiness, at least this time. If soup is now too cool, return to the pan just to heat through again.

Just before serving, warm a little olive oil, about a tablespoon and stir a little more pounded saffron into it, in the microwave works best if you have one. If not, be very, very careful not to let the oil get too hot, or to let the saffron burn.

Divide the soup into bowls, with a spoonful of popped corn carefully on top, so it doesn't sink and disappear into the soup, a drizzle of the amber hued, saffron oil as finishing touch - and waste not a moment in eating.

Celeriac and Porcini Gratin with Star Anise and Brandy

I've heard celeriac referred to as the ugliest vegetable in the world, which makes me want to jump to its defence at once. *"I love you greedily!"* I want to sing to it. *"You may seem lumpen and hard-headed, gnarled and earth bound as a withered old stump but I know your deep secrets."* It's true that celeriac needs a little coaxing to reveal all of its subtle, earthen, primal sweetness. It can be robust in a soup, tantalisingly sweet in a Remoulade, the endlessly appealing French way with mayonnaise, a sophisticated slaw if ever there were. I have sliced it paper thin and used the blanched slices in lieu of pasta to make ricotta and almond-filled cannelloni (perhaps in the next edition). Wrapped in foil, slathered in butter and mustard and herbs and garlic, then roasted in a slow oven for a couple of hours, it feeds an informal crowd, more seasonings by the side, spoons at the ready for communal attack. It makes a divine mash, on its own or mixed with potatoes and soft, roasted garlic, olive or truffle oil. It adds delicate intrigue to a tray of roasted roots and it makes this delectable, stove-top gratin. Parsley and mushrooms are natural allies, as is orange, especially the oven dried peel, blitzed to a coarse powder.

For hard-headed fact rather than fanciful musings, it is of course the cultivated root of celery. If you grow it yourself, or buy it at the farmer's market, you will see the baby branches of celery beginning to shoot through the top. The French for it is Céleri–Rave, something I had completely forgotten till I came to live in Paris and met with blank stares when I used the English word, convinced that it was French.

For best results, you'll need to let caramelisation happen. You'll need to step back occasionally yet remain present, stirring sometimes, letting it do its thing for a minute or two, before engaging with it again. It's that balance between pushing things almost to the edge when they start to catch, stick to the pan and even come close to burning, releasing natural sugars, then intervening with a dash more liquid, a quick stir, a flash of heat or a gentle adjustment. It's hard to predict exactly how it will go for you, hard to give precise cooking times, but think of the heat itself as a magical element and you as the magician dancing a magical fire dance. Because when it's done right the celeriac will let you have everything it's got. And that's a lot.

Celeriac and Porcini Gratin

Serves 4 - 6

Ingredients

20g dried porcini mushrooms, soaked as described below

¼ tsp tamari or soya sauce

dash tabasco

1 tbs brandy

2 tbs olive oil

small onion, or 1 shallot finely sliced, optional

1 whole celeriac, peeled and cleaned

½ lemon, optional

3 garlic cloves, finely sliced

150 ml double cream

a small bundle of chives, snipped super-small

60g gruyere, shredded to a fine thread

sea salt and freshly ground black pepper

Method

Start by soaking the Porcini mushrooms in a marinade composed of the Tamari, or soya sauce, the Tabasco, brandy, and about 600 ml hot water. You can do this overnight and certainly at least an hour beforehand.

Strain and keep the liquid - think of it as black gold - and discard the debris. Use your fingers to double check that there is no more grit trapped in the mushrooms. Set aside.

It's probably easiest to cut the peeled celeriac into quarters, before slicing into slices not quite iphone thick – say 2 – 3 mm. If you are not going to go straight into the recipe, then make sure to squeeze lemon juice all over the slices to prevent browning.

Otherwise, fry the shallot or onion in half the hot oil. When golden brown, add the remaining oil til hot and then the slices of celeriac and the sliced garlic. Toss and turn on a medium heat to coat in the oniony oil. I find it best to let the celeriac sit undisturbed for a minute or two, so it just begins to catch on the bottom of the pan, then to use a spatula to gently ease it off the bottom, turn it, let it sit, repeat the motion. So some of the cooking does itself but you are aiding it along as necessary.
After about ten minutes of this and as the celeriac begins to soften and show streaks of gold, add the Porcini and the stock, perhaps not all at once. Adjust the heat if necessary, let it simmer till very tender, one or two pieces can even be falling apart but not too much. You will probably have used up all the stock but if there's a little left, keep it for soup, or freeze it.

At the last minute, add the cream and stir gently. With the snipped chives stirred through, it's good enough to eat as it is but a shower of grated Gruyère all over and under a hot grill for a few minutes adds the golden burnish we all love so much.

Red Chicory Salad with Roquefort and Clementine Dressing with Walnuts

Funny how three intrinsically bitter ingredients can work as harmoniously as these but the Roquefort, endive and walnuts do just that. As in the braised chicory recipe that follows, citrus rounds everything off, as do the Dijon mustard and the dash of chili. The more usual thing is to crumble most of the Roquefort into the salad and to add the remainder to an olive oil and vinegar dressing.

I've cut out a step and done away with most of the oil, in what's already a pretty full on dressing. It isn't the prettiest colour but nothing that can't be zhuzhed up. Just chop a small handful of flat leaf parsley or chives and stir into the dressing together with the orange or clementine zest before pouring it over. The striated claret and white endive leaves are almost like an exotic orchid's petals, so though easier to eat if you slice them to slivers, since we also eat with our eyes, I prefer to leave them intact.

Ingredients

4 - 6 whole red chicory, tough end sliced off, leaves separated
6 whole walnuts, shelled or 12 walnut halves

Dressing

100g roquefort, or any other, sharp, salty blue cheese to your taste
¼ small red onion, chopped very small
juice and zest of 1 clementine
2 tbs boiling water
1 tsp dijon mustard
dash tabasco, or other chili sauce
dash sweet white vinegar
handful flat leaf parsley or chives, finely chopped
½ tbs walnut oil, optional
¼ tsp cracked black pepper

Method

Bring a kettle to the boil. Place the separated leaves in a bowl and set aside for a minute.

Then crumble the roquefort into a small bowl. Add the boiling water and stir to melt the cheese. Add the remaining ingredients, including herbs. Stir and pour all over the leaves. Scatter walnuts atop and serve.

Tête à Tête

Roasted Parsnips with a Petit Pois Velouté, Roasted Pear and Parsnip and Petit Pois Fritters

I wanted something French and elegant, rich but not impossibly so, pretty and sophisticated but easy and fun to make. Parsnips aren't very French but for a few brief weeks, they were at the downstairs market, small and super fresh and as for petit pois, if that's not French, what is?

Then there's the butter and the wine and the touch of brandy. It's all rather unexpected but it works as a starter, where soup might have gone. I've given you small portions. Very French. (A dark rye bread cleans the plate by the way.) Whichever way you go, I strongly suggest that you please serve with a salad of baby gem lettuces – you'll need two for 4 portions, tossed together with a very crisp Lebanese cucumber, peeled and sliced paper thin, a glug of olive oil and a smaller, one of a sweet wine vinegar, or Balsamic "condiment", a word I can only bring myself to use in inverted commas, plus a little sea salt and freshly ground black pepper.

Double up if you want this as a main course and also add a side of green beans or tender stem broccoli with toasted almonds.

A little tip here from the Japanese, rather than the French kitchen, everyone could easily adopt: whisk the egg with a pair of chopsticks to break it up, add the water and whisk again. Use them again to beat in the flour – and here's the best bit – and again to drop the fritters into the hot oil and lift them out again! Isn't that neat!!

Quartered baby gem lettuce in a rich mustardy vinagrette goes beautifully with it.

P.S. When deep frying, I learnt early on to always have a lid and a damp tea towel to hand, just as safety precautions. But mostly to keep a vigilant eye on the hot oil - I once paid a very heavy price for not doing so.

Roasted Parsnips with a Petit Pois Velouté, Roasted Pear and Parsnip and Petit Pois Fritters

Serves 2 - 4

Ingredients

For the Parsnips

350g parsnips - about one smallish per person

4 cloves garlic, left whole in the skin

dash tabasco

salt and pepper

For the Pears

1 williams pear, ripe but firm, cut into 8 segments, core removed

15g butter

1 tsp brandy

freshly ground black pepper

1 long red chilli

sea salt and freshly ground black pepper

For the Petit Pois Velouté

1 shallot or ½ small red onion

1 small clove garlic, chopped very small

125g frozen best possible quality petit pois, blanched in salted boiling water for one minute, then immediately refreshed under cold water, reserving one full cup of the blanching water

35g butter, divided

2 sprigs flat leaf parsley, or basil, picked off the stalks

juice of half a lime, or 2 tbs white wine

½ tbs fruity olive oil

sea salt and white pepper

For the Fritters

line a plate with two layers of kitchen paper towels and set aside

2 whole parsnips, peeled and shredded

125g frozen petit pois, thawed in boiling water and immediately refreshed under cold water

For the Fritter batter

125g plain white flour

125g corn flour

225ml (1 cup) ice - cold sparkling water

1 egg white, lightly beaten

zest of 1 lime

sea salt and freshly ground black pepper

½ thumb long red chilli, seeds removed, chopped small

To Fry

750 ml sunflower, or other flavourless oil

To serve

dark rye bread

Method

Preheat the oven to 200°C/Fan 180°C/Gas 6.

Shred the parsnips for the fritters and mix with the petit pois, season with salt and pepper and set aside for now.

Now cut the whole parsnips into quarters, or sixths if they are on the big side, and place on a tray with the whole garlic cloves. Add 1 tbsp of olive oil, salt, pepper, a dash of Tabasco and toss to coat.

Place in the hot oven and roast for 35 minutes,til browned, completely tender and beginning to caramelise, even shrivel a little.

Meanwhile, fry the finely chopped shallot or onion and garlic in 10g of butter til completely soft but making sure that it does not colour at all. This is so that the velouté stays as bright a green as possible. At the last minute, wilt a couple of sprigs of flat leaf parsley into the onion mixture. Remove from heat, add to the petit pois and blend with the reserved blanching water til very smooth and velvety.

Transfer back to the pan and slowly bring back to the boil, adding the white wine or lime juice and the remaining 25g butter, a little at a time, stirring continuously and finally the half tablespoon of olive oil. It sounds like too little to make a difference but it adds a necessary silkiness.

Now cut the 8 pear segments into 2 cm pieces and the chili into long, thin quarters, heat the butter in a frying pan with the brandy and sautée the pear til appealingly golden on all sides, adding the chili to the pan so that it also softens. Remove from heat and set aside.

Ten minutes or so before you are ready to serve, make the fritters: heat the sunflower oil in a small pan, making sure the oil reaches no further than half way up the side of the pan at most.

Sift the flours into a bowl, add the salt, lime zest and chili, then add the cold sparkling water and finally the lightly beaten egg white. Use immediately. For best results keep the batter cold, even as you are working with it, by setting it over another bowl containing ice cubes.

Mix all the raw parsnip and thawed petit pois into the batter, mix well and drop spoonfuls, two or three at a time, no more, into the hot oil, taking great care that the oil doesn't bubble up too fast and adjusting the heat accordingly. It mustn't get too cool or the fritters will go soggy, or too hot so that they burn before being cooked through. Watch like a hawk.

Use the chopsticks to lift the fritters out when they are golden brown and with no trace of raw batter. Transfer to the paper lined plate, and season with a little more salt while still very hot.

To Plate

Have some wide bowls at the ready.

Warm the pea velouté through for a minute, then carefully spoon just two tablespoons of it into each bowl. Place 4 or 5 pieces of roasted parsnips on top, loosely as in the children's game, pick-up sticks. Dot the roasted pear around, five or six pieces per plate. Finally crown with a fritter each (you will have spares!) and a little of the soft red chili, whose skin should have loosened and fallen off.

Braised Chicory with Hot Smoked Salmon

The inclusion of this obviously not vegetarian recipe is an accurate reflection of the non-vegetarian to vegetarian ratio in my own diet – about 5% of the time, I may well eat a little piece of fish, even more rarely a piece of meat. You may wonder why I don't just give up this small amount altogether to maintain my vegetarian credentials, but over the years I have found that it is much easier for me to stick to a very largely vegetarian diet by not imposing blanket strictures on myself. That works for me and I think I am old enough to know.

The French have long understood the appeal of chicory (what they call endive) and I've loved it since childhood, dressed in a sharp mustard vinaigrette with walnuts and snipped chives, sometimes braised and sometimes as a gratin with Gruyere. Most of the cooking at home was rather predictably done by my mother who had learnt very late to cook and who by nature would have lived on soup and salad (and dark chocolate) but my father was definitely the final arbiter of taste. He would come into the kitchen and make final adjustments and irritating as that might sound, I must admit that he really did have an extraordinary knack for it. Two things stay in my mind. For one, he would insist that the "gôut soit rond", that the taste be rounded and for two, soupçon was a favourite word. I'm pretty sure that I've inherited from him this instinct to add sometimes only infinitesimal amounts of something to seek balance and harmony in my cooking.

So I knew that the bitterness of the chicory would need to be balanced by a little sweetness, a little acidity, a little warmth and orange is what did it.

Braised Chicory with Hot Smoked Salmon

Serves 2 - 4

Ingredients

500g chicory - about 6, very small ones left whole, larger ones cut in half along the length

30g butter

zest of about half an orange

¼ large orange, juice only

75 ml hot water

1 garlic clove, very finely sliced

4 long chives, snipped teeny, weeny

½ tsp rice vinegar, or some other sweet, mild, white wine vinegar

250g piece hot smoked salmon, skin removed

1 tbs double cream

Herbamare or regular salt

cracked black or pink pepper

Method

Melt the 30g butter in a medium saucepan but do not let it brown. The beauty is all in the paleness.

Trim the thinnest possible slice off the end of the chicory so that it stays intact, even when cut in half.

Lower into the butter and again keep the heat low and as much as possible, do not let brown, though a little caramelisation at the end and just on the tips is inevitable and good.

Add the 75 ml of hot water, the rice vinegar, the herbamare or regular salt and cracked black or pink pepper. Ensure heat is at a murmur, place a lid on the pan and simmer very gently for 35 - 40 minutes, turning regularly and making sure the liquid is not running dry, though you do want it to reduce, so it does little more than coat the chicory with only a spoonful or two to spare and it is marvelously tender.

In the last minutes, add the spoon of double cream and the orange juice and zest. Move the pan about, so it all comes together fluidly and easily and in the last 2 minutes place the salmon on top, just to take away the cold, not to further cook it.

Scatter the finely snipped chives all over and divide into 2 plates, 4 as a small starter or part of a meal composed of many elements.

Index

First published by Trajectory Books 2020
This edition Trajectory Books ISBN 978-1-8381176-1-0

This book is typeset in Raleway and Libre Baskerville with titles in Libre Baskerville.
The named type families are available from Google.
Author's website: nadinesfeast.com
Photographer's website: karenhb.co.uk
Publisher's website: trajectorybooks.com

TRAJECTORY BOOKS

Printed in Great Britain
by Amazon